The Road Upward

By Je' Czaja

Table of Contents

I Have the Power to Choose..Section1, Page 3
My Choices Affect Others..Section 2, Page 7
My Worldview..Section 3, Page 11
I Have to Wake Up Before I Can See..........................Section 4, Page 17
Growing Up..Section 5, Page 23
There is Only One God...Section 6, Page 28
Life is So Daily..Section 7, Page 32
If I Keep Doing What I've Done..............................Section 8, Page 36
I Reap What I Sow..Section 9, Page 40
Forgive to Set Yourself Free.....................................Section 10, Page 43
I Have Done Some Rotten Things.............................Section 11, Page 48
The Big Questions...Section 12, Page 50

I HAVE THE POWER TO CHOOSE: GOOD OR BAD

This course is about you living a good life. We might say, "Man, she's living the good life," and we usually mean she is living in wealth and luxury. Or we might say, "Johnathan has lived a good life," and we mean something very different.

What is the difference between living "the good life" and living "a good life?"

Some values are universal; all people, everywhere, hold them. Some of these are generosity, telling the truth, loyalty to family and friends and cooperation. Everyone recognizes some Ultimate Value. It might be love, truth, beauty, justice, reason, nature or God, (defined as a being containing all these things in the highest form.)

We know that love, truth, and fairness (justice) exist here on earth on different levels. They are not material, but they are real. Some people seem to be more and some less, loving, truthful, or fair and that may vary from time to time. God is all these qualities in constant and extreme form, Ultimate Love, Truth and Fairness, for example.

God, by definition, is Ultimate Love, Truth, Beauty and Justice.
These good things exist.
Therefore God exists.

We may have to suspend our disbelief at times to learn new ideas and that is no big deal; we do it whenever we watch a cartoon. When the cartoon mouse blows up the cartoon cat, we don't complain,"Nonsense. That bomb would have killed that cat." We "suspend our disbelief." We do this all the time.

Universal laws are not "Thou shalt nots," they are the truth about the way things work. They are a bit like the law of gravity. You can defy the law of gravity by jumping off a fifteen story building, but it will have a bad result for you. Right?

Gravity is a physical law, it always works here on earth. You can drop a brick over your foot to test this. What happens? You can try to break the law of gravity, but you will break yourself instead. You can break the Universal laws, too, and you will be the one broken.

My choices have consequences. Good or bad.

Jack and Jill

Maria

Trevor

**The road of life winds upward for the wise
that he may escape the pit below**

Discussion Questions: Look at the picture...

1. Who has made it? How does she feel?
2. Who is in the process of making it? Has this been difficult?
3. Trevor hit an obstacle and fell off. What does he have to do now?
4. Why don't many people even start on the road upward?

It seems to be hard for most people, especially people whose lives are not working well, to admit three things:

1. I can be wrong. 2, I don't know everything. 3. I need help sometimes.

I CAN BE _____.

I_____ _____ EVERYTHING.

I _____ _____ SOMETIMES.

Have you ever changed your mind about something? Then obviously, you can be wrong. Has life ever hit you with a burden too heavy to bear alone? Did others help you?

Have you ever chosen to do a rotten thing? Did God stop you? Why not?

Section Two

My Choices Affect Others

Curtis raped a twelve year-old girl when he was sixteen. He ended up in jail. Curtis made a _____ choice and got a _____ consequence. His bad choice hurt himself, but he was not the only one.

What suffering has Curtis' bad choice caused:

Himself?
The girl?
His parents?
His siblings?
His friends?
His society?

We have no choice over our birth circumstances and very little over our death circumstances, but in between these two events, we have billions of choices. Viktor Frankl wrote *Man's Search for Meaning*, about time he spent in a Nazi work camp. As a psychiatrist, he was a trained observer of human behavior. He concluded:

"Everything can be taken from a man but one thing: the last of the human freedoms—to choose one's attitude in any given set of circumstances, to choose one's own way."

But what if someone has a gun to your head and says, "Do this or I'll shoot!" Do you have any choice then?

"How we spend our days is, of course, how we spend our lives."-Anne Dillard

Whatever we have done or what has been done to us, we are still alive and can change. True or False?

The eternal laws can tell us the right way to turn. They are the truth about how the world works. Some **relativists** say there are no eternal laws, it is all relative. **But do something rotten to a relativist and they act as if there are eternal laws after all.**

**You lied!
No I didn't. I just didn't
tell all the truth.**

**I lent your rent money.
You never paid me back!**

It's all relative.

Tamburi

In Tamburi a group of men decided they were free to do whatever they wanted. They invaded homes, shot the men, raped the women, ate all the food and stole all the valuables. They lied and betrayed each other and assassinated each other, because they all wanted to be the head honcho.

How long do you think this free society will last? If each person did whatever he wanted with no regard for others, that society would self-destruct. True or false?

Our choices affect us first, then ripple out and affect those closest to us, those close to them and on and on. A choice is like tossing a pebble into a pond, sending out ripples. At the same time, their choices are affecting us.

C.S. Lewis: There are two ways in which the human machine goes wrong. One is when human individuals...collide with one another and do one another damage, by cheating or bullying. The other is when things go wrong inside the individual-when the different parts of him...drift apart or interfere with each other.

Think of a fleet sailing in formation. The voyage will be a success only, if in the first place, the ships do not collide with each other...and secondly if each ship is seaworthy. As a matter of fact, you cannot have either of these things without the other. If the ships keep on colliding they will not remain seaworthy for long. On the other hand, if their steering gears are out of order they will not be able to avoid collision.

Individuals are important, but they live in societies, which are also important; it is not either/or, it is both. Jesus dealt with individuals in very personal ways. But the criteria for judging his followers was how they treated each other. "Whatever you do for the least of these, you do for me."

Section 3

My Worldview

How do you think the world would looks to an earthworm?

How about to a dog?

How about to a religious astronaut?

They may see the world very differently, though it is the same world. You, too, have a unique worldview made up of all the things you have heard, seen and experienced. In fact, there never has and never will be a person exactly like you.
So how valuable are you?

Besides our unique worldview, we are born with a temperament. We are rowdy or quiet or thoughtful or orderly and any mother can tell you we are born that way, with a temperament, or a tendency to act in certain (usually) predictable ways. What is your temperament? There are lots of personality tests, but this very simple one should do.

The **OTTER** is playful, friendly, and sociable. An otter may talk a lot, be the life of the party and be everybody's friend. The other temperaments may think the otter is shallow, not very loyal, and not very "deep." They get angry quickly and get over it just as quickly. They feel energized being in a crowd, whereas other temperaments may feel drained by crowds.

The bulldog is a born leader; he is the Prussian general of temperaments. They are driven, they persevere, they expect a lot of themselves and demand a lot from others. They have a vision they intend to bring to pass. The other temperaments may think the bulldog is too harsh and bossy, and he may be. They get angry and don't forget it. They may get revenge years later. They need a crowd, if only to order around.

The panther is quiet and may seem moody. They like to think and are often artistically gifted. They don't like crowds so much. They can explode with anger and lash out. They may stay mad, too, whenever they think about it again. They are very loyal friends. They think the otter is silly and the bulldog is mean.

The tortoise is dependable. He is apt to enjoy routine and paperwork, which he will fill out completely and with a smile. He doesn't like crowds because they are rather distracting and disorderly. He gets mad and does a slow burn for a long time. They are easy to get along with and the bulldog needs them, the otter likes to tease them, and the panther appreciates their being quiet.

Which are you? Maybe you say, "Mostly otter and a bit bulldog." That's normal, we usually have a primary and secondary temperament. Your temperament helps you understand yourself a little better and also helps you understand other people. They may not be lazy or uncaring, they may just be a tortoise.

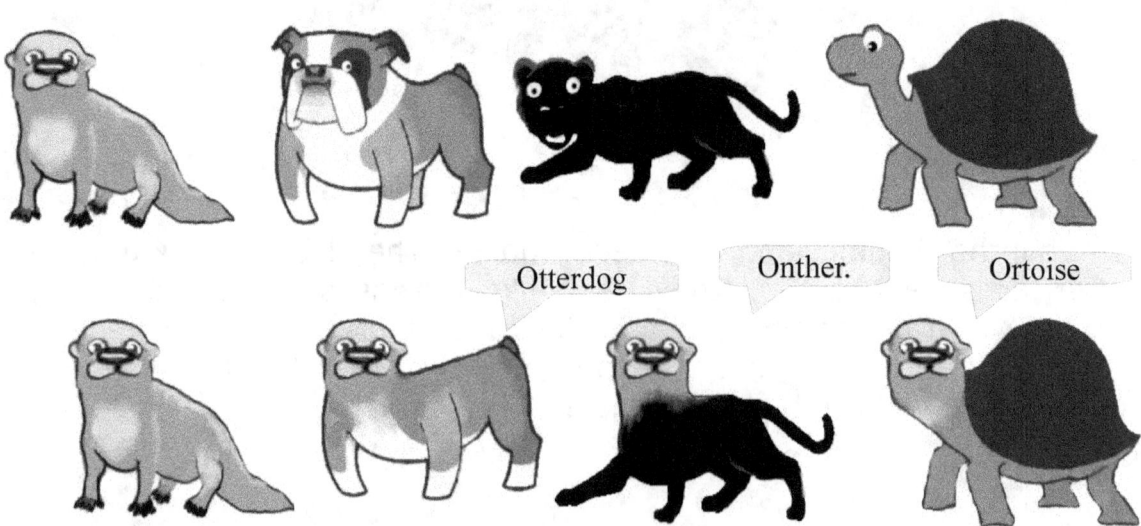

Otterdog   Onther.   Ortoise

But don't use it as an excuse, either, for bad behavior. "I'm not mean, I'm just a bulldog." A bulldog doesn't have to be mean; in fact, being mean defeats the bulldog. He wants to get things done and meanness isn't the best way to get things done.

So at a party the otter is romping around, the bulldog is recruiting followers and the panther and tortoise are in the corner, wishing they were at home.

At what job might an otter excel? A bulldog? A panther? A tortoise? At what job might you excel?

Have you ever been frustrated with someone who didn't think just like you?

Each person has their unique worldview, but that is, of course, influenced by those around us. If our culture (a blend of our history, language and customs) says the most important thing is making money, we are apt to think so, too. If it says the most important thing is caring for your parents (China's filial piety) we are apt to think so, too. If it says the most important thing is maintaining the current class structure, we are apt to think so, too.

But what is the most important thing to you?

Is it possible that someone's worldview, or parts of it, could be wrong? Some say it doesn't matter what you believe as long as you are sincere. Is that true? What if you sincerely believe you can fly and jump off the Grand Canyon?

"Keep an open mind, but not so open that your brains fall out."

You have to start right where you are. Where else could you start?

Section 4

I Have to Wake up Before I Can See

Plato was a philosopher who lived a few hundred years before Christ. Plato (Broad shoulders) was his nickname; maybe he worked out a lot. One of his questions concerned a magic invisibility ring you could put on at will. If you were invisible, would you rob a bank? Why or why not?

One of his most famous stories is about the cave, a metaphor for seeing what is real. He says we are all chained in a cave with a fire behind us and all we see is flickering shadows on the cave wall in front of us. We think that's all there is.

But what if you broke the chains and went outside and saw the sun and trees and colors? What if you went to free the others and told them there is a whole other world and it's brighter and richer? Do you think they would go with you? Or do you think they would say you're crazy?

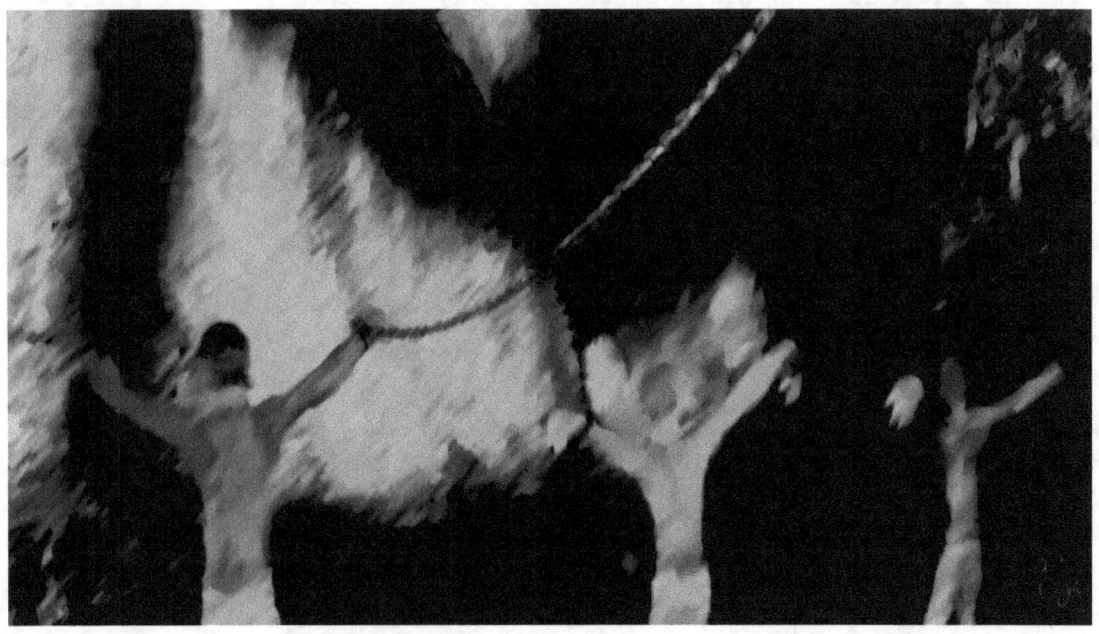

A Tale of the South

Midville is a rural county in the south. The banks and medical forms provide a place for your X because 25% of the 15,000 people in Midville are illiterate. Most people in Midville are poor. Do you think Midville has a high crime rate? Why or why not?

About one hundred years ago Jack Reid married Penny. Jack was mean when he was drunk and he took it out on Penny and the five children. Penny came from a family where she was unloved and treated like a slave. She couldn't wait to get out and married the first man who asked her. She grew to hate Jack and the kids grew to hate them both.

Jerome Starnes married Maria and they actually loved each other. They had six kids and were delighted with them. Though they did not have more money than the Reids, they had a good life.

If you could rate people 0-10, 10 being very evil, how would you rate

1. Jack Reid?
2. His wife, Penny?
3. Jerome Starnes?

Why?

The Reids produced 105 children in 100 years, the Starnes produced 106.

1. How many Reids and Starnes do you think abused alcohol?
2. How many Reids and Starnes finished high school?
3. How many Reids and Starnes went to jail? Why?

Do you think any Starnes turned out to be addicts or criminals? Why or why not?

Do you think any Reids turned out well? Why or why not?

In Midville, people said the Reids had "Bad blood." Is there such a thing as bad blood?

What it's like to live at the Reids:

What it's like to live at the Starnes:

Personal Growth

We're here to grow; to germinate, grow toward the light and flower.
We are here to flourish.

1. The first step is to see it.
2. The second step is to want it.
3. The third step is to do it. Nobody can do it for you.

Raymond Reid had a bad childhood. His dad died of cirrhosis of the liver when he was eight and his mom has had a string of loser boyfriends ever since. Raymond just got out of juvenile detention.

His dad is dead. Can he change anything now?
His mom is alive. Can she change anything now?
Raymond is on the wrong path. Can he change anything now?

This is the tape that plays in Raymond's head. You answer it.

1. I'm a Reid, there's no hope for me.

2. Men drink. I'm a man, so I drink.
3. No matter what, I'm doomed.

That last one is a lie, but strangely, believing a lie has almost as much power as believing the truth. People growing up in abusive homes have sometimes learned helplessness. And they can un-learn it.

Carl knew he had a few problems, but he thought they were just bad luck. He had a lousy job, his wife was always mad at him, his kids disrespected him, and he was always in debt. One day he turned off the TV commercial, and actually thought. "Hang on, I could do something about my bad luck. I could make some choices here, just as soon as I win the lottery, its all going to be O.K. Then he turned on the TV, thinking, "Yup, as soon as I win the lottery." He would pick up a ticket that afternoon.

What mistake is Carl making?

1. He needs several lottery tickets, not just one.

2. He should call the Psychic Hotline to get the winning numbers.
3. He has to start now, where he is, not where he might someday be.
4. None of the above, Carl is just unlucky.

I AM RESPONSIBLE FOR WHAT I THINK.

I AM RESPONSIBLE FOR WHAT I SAY.

I AM RESPONSIBLE TO TEACH OTHERS HOW I WANT TO BE TREATED.

I AM RESPONSIBLE FOR MY RELATIONSHIPS.

I AM RESPONSIBLE TO TREAT OTHERS AS I WANT TO BE TREATED.

Shon is a workaholic. He works all week then brings his work home and works late into the night and all weekend. Charlie chases physical pleasures, comfort food, women and whatever gives him a buzz. Shon and Charlie are UNBALANCED.

A theory of virtues (which means strengths) says virtues exist along a line from too much to too little to just right-the balance. It is not wrong to work or seek pleasure. It is the extremes that cause misery.

This is Aristotle's (and other's) idea of the Golden Mean. You might call it the Mountain in the Middle. Any virtue taken to extremes can become become evil.

Can you think of some others?

Recklessness.....Courage............Cowardice
Needy................Satisfied.............Greedy

Are either Shon or Charlie happy? Do they have any lasting peace? What can they do to fix this?

Section 5

Growing Up

Two year-olds are about as cute as they can be. One mom said God made them cute so we wouldn't kill them. Why would she say this? Because two year-olds show us human nature in the raw.

Two year-olds are convinced they are the center of the universe. Everyone and everything exists to please them. They are thoroughly selfish. But that's O.K. Because they are only two years-old; they are going to outgrow it.

Or are they?

Watch what happens with a room full of people and a two year-old. They will show off, make noise, and do anything to make the people look at them. After all, they are the center of the universe, what's wrong with those tall people?

They want stuff. They want it now, they aren't going to wait, they aren't going to earn it, they don't even think how inconvenient it might be for other people. They are apt to handle offenses by biting. But that's O.K. They are two years-old. Let's face it, a forty year who acts like this is just a jerk.

Lest we think two year-olds are all bad remember: They are cute, they can be sweet and they are honest. And when they say, "I love you," they mean it.

I was in a grocery store with someone who I loved. Suddenly he grabbed my face in both hands and bit me on the cheek. We continued toward the cereal aisle. He didn't explain or apologize. People were staring; I felt a bit self-conscious.

Then he started clapping and slapped me in the face. A few minutes later, he looked very serious and threw up all over my shirt. Is this guy psycho? Why would I tolerate this abuse? Because he was my year-old son.

Behavior that is normal for toddlers is unacceptable from adults. We're supposed to grow up.

Grown ups are expected to think about the long-term results of their choices. They are supposed to say, "Wait a minute, if I do that, what might happen?" The fancy name for that is impulse control and we don't develop it until we are adults and some people never seem to develop it very highly.

Wait a minute; if I do that, what might happen?

1. How might impulse control prevent arrests?

2. **How might impulse control prevent injury?**
3. **How might impulse control prevent death?**

Plato said we should wake up and at some point we should grow up. Socrates said we should also examine our life. He got the death sentence for running around Athens encouraging people to do this. He said, "The un-examined life is not worth living."

What did he mean by that? You have probably known some smart dogs, but you never knew a dog who did this:

The dog just eats when he's hungry and drinks when he's dry. You might say he is dogmatic in his thinking. He runs on autopilot.

Are you dogmatic?
Or do you, every now and then-THINK?

Overheard: Every time I tell people to think for themselves, they act like I told them to sit naked on a hot stove.

Worrying is a waste of time.

But what if...? But then, what if....? That's what worriers do and they answer the question with the worst possible outcome. Then they feel stressed and get analysis paralysis. And so do nothing.

The thing I greatly feared is come upon me. (Job 3:25)

How many things have you worried about like this actually happened? Almost none. Then worrying was a waste of time.
And for the tiny number of things you worried about that did happen, your worrying didn't prevent them. So worrying is a total waste of time.

Who of you by worrying can add a single hour to his lifespan? (Matthew 6:27)

Here's what you can do instead: If you start worrying, stop it and PLAN instead. If A happens, then I will do B. If B happens, then I will do C. Do this every time you start worrying, because worrying is a waste of time, but planning is not.

SWOT: Serious Planning

People don't need a SWOT plan for every decision, but for big, long-range planning, SWOT provides a framework. Be sure to review your SWOT plans, because the old world keep on changing, little by little, and you will want to adjust it.

S=Strengths
W=Weaknesses
O=Obstacles
T=Threats

There is Only One God
(and you are not Him)

Pretty close though

Some angry atheists think they have found the one thing that causes problems throughout history and that one thing is religion. In this false and simplistic view, all you have to do is get rid of religion and everything will be fine. (Either that, or they have daddy issues.) I was an atheist for a number of years, until I realized that God can't be proven or disproven with logic or philosophy, so I called myself agnostic, which means "I do not know."

There are lots of decent atheists, but the new, angry ones are merely saying, "What I have chosen to believe is better than what you have chosen to believe. Because I'm smart and you are stupid." They say that religion has caused all the suffering in the world, and when that is wiped out, there will be no more suffering in the world.

Easily refuted: The Bolsheviks were official and vehement atheists, killed millions, and spent decades trying to wipe out theism with violence. Ironically, now the statues of the Bolshevik leaders have been taken down and stored...in a church basement.

Angry atheists even slammed Mother Teresa, saying, basically, she was not perfect. She would have been the first to agree with that assessment. The angry atheists, who sometimes suggest Christianity is child abuse (and perhaps Christian parents should be jailed and the children raised by the state?) are just jealous because their shelter in Calcutta was better than Mother Teresa's. Oh, they have no shelter in Calcutta? New York? Then they need to get a life and go volunteer to help their community instead of airing their silly ideas. Sorry for the rant, but they are harming people.

You may be familiar with Twelve Step programs that ask you to choose your higher power. Because everyone has one, everyone has an Ultimate Value: Love, Truth, Beauty, Nature, Goodness or the Ultimate Everything we call God. God, by definition, encompasses all these good things in the highest form.

What are good things? We humans usually think in three dimensional terms and say good things are things that contribute to our health or well-being. Things that do not we call bad. Good is what we call a thing that does what it is designed to do; a pen is good if it writes smoothly, a knife is good is it cuts effortlessly, pie is good if the filling is just right and the crust if flaky.

But what is a good person? What is a person designed to do? According to anthropolgist Donald Brown, all humans everywhere share some things in common. Two of these are forbidding rape and murder. Yet obviously rape and murder occur! These two universals illustrate what philosophers call the Human Problem. That is, we do not even live up to the standards we set for ourselves!

We sin. The original meaning of sin is to miss the target. There is a target and we miss it. We are unlikely to hit the target if we are not looking at the target. We will not hit the target if we don't pay attention to it or if we pretend the target does not exist. The target in this case is a rape and murder-free society.

Because we miss that target, shall we say it's a bad target? Or do we need to try again, because it's a good target? Our conscience may not be a perfect guide, but we all have one. We all feel bad when we do something rotten, unless we have denied our own conscience so many times that sin has become painless.

Let's say we want to live in a rape-free and murder-free society. We will never hit the target if we refuse to LOOK at the target.

What other qualities would we like in a society? In ourselves?

Why are we here? We are here to grow our soul. That is success, not world fame or billions in our stock portfolio. Then we have peace in any circumstances. Then we grow; then we flourish as we were meant to flourish.

Section 7

Life Is So Daily

Take a minute to think back on your day today. You woke up, went to the bathroom, maybe got a cup of coffee. Then you got dressed, maybe drove to work...what else?

How much of your day did you run on autopilot? Maybe when you were little you had to think about each button you buttoned, or when you learned to drive, you were very alert to dangers, but now you probably did those things without much thought.

Philosophers want us to be **rational**, by which they mean they want us to weigh and judge all our actions and choose the best one. But even philosophers run on autopilot most of the time, and while we know we can be rational, we seldom bother to do it. Autopilot works fine most of the time, otherwise we wouldn't be alive and reading this.

In the olden days, they said that emotions (they called them passions) clouded our rationality and while they didn't know then that everybody must use emotions to think at all, they proved the necessity of emotions to thinking by using very emotional appeals against emotions. Emotions were stupid, barbaric, and deadly.

The Mountain in the Middle acknowledges that emotions are part of being human, just like the ability to make rational judgments. "In your anger, do not sin," the Bible says. You will feel anger but what you choose to do next determines if you hit the target or miss the target (i.e. sin.) If you kill the person with whom you are angry, you have sinned. But what if they are really rotten?

True story: A man came home from work early and found his wife in bed with his friend. This is the kind of thing that makes one very angry. He got his gun and made them stay in bed, then made two phone calls.

First he called his wife's mother and told her to get over there immediately. The mother did come and saw the situation. Then he called the police and told them they also needed to get over there immediately. He was both emotional and rational. It can be done! No doubt we all do it, sometimes.

Emotions can be painful. We don't like pain; why would we? Dr. Paul Brand worked with people who could feel no pain and wrote a book, *Pain: The Gift No One Wants.* It seems that pain is necessary, it warns us that something should change. He tells of one of his patients who ran on a broken ankle, ended up running on his leg bone and never felt it. His patients wore off their extremities because they could not feel pain.

Pain is a way of telling us that something should change.

Thoughts can be painful. The bible instructs us to "take our thoughts captive." How does that work? We can't choose what to think, can we? Actually, we can.

Anyone who has ever been clinically depressed knows your thoughts can kill you. If they are that powerful, can they also make you well? But how do you capture them?

NOT by **trying <u>not</u> to think** about it, but by **replacing** that painful thought with a better one. Try not thinking of an elephant. Go ahead. Somehow, elephant keeps coming back. Now read this:

The sun is rising on another steamy day in the deep jungle. A tea-colored river winds through the lush greenery-But look! A raccoon is ambling down the beach to get a drink of water. But oh no, he doesn't see the yellow eyes of the hungry, submerged crocodile waiting for him.

The elephant you were contemplating has been replaced. This works with negative thoughts, too. Try it. Gather up a bunch of good

34

thoughts for emergencies. When you start to think bad, pull out a good one and focus on that. We all have losses. Focus on what you still have instead of what you have lost.

What do you still have that is good? Make a list.

If I Keep on Doing What I've Done
I'll Keep on Getting What I've Got

This was a poster on a counselor's office wall. We assume if people went to him for help, they did not like what they had got. They will have to something different.

Insanity: Doing the same thing over and over and expecting a different result.

Surely we have all done that, but why? Here's another:

Until the pain of changing becomes greater than the pain of staying the same, we will not change.

Is that true?

> Jan and Richard were miserable. This was the second marriage for both and they didn't want to go through another divorce. Jan's first husband was an alcoholic and she didn't want another one. Richard's first wife was a nag and he didn't want another one. Within a year he was drinking and she was nagging. He said he drank because she nagged him and she said she nagged him because he drank.

What can they do to get un-stuck?

Most people assume that the way things were in their FOO, their Family of Origin, are normal. It is one of many things they can argue about.

Many people had a bad childhood so they decide they will fix their FOO by re-enacting the whole mess, only this time they will do it <u>right.</u> Maybe they were neglected, so they will lavish affection on THEIR kids and thereby Fix their FOO.

Do you think this will work?

We all have a past and we can't change it. True story: An attractive woman who had just got out of prison said she didn't let the past bother her, she just threw it in the back seat and drove down the road. Another pointed out, "But if it's in the back seat, then it's going with you wherever you go."

The Past will not be different.

Will the present? Will the future? Maybe the past was not up to you, but to a great extent the present and the future are up to you.

The Amazing Power of Belief

We all believe many things, some weakly and some strongly and some in between. We believe them based on testimony from others, or from our senses, or from personal experience. Testimony from others can be wrong and our senses can be wrong, but we choose to believe a whole bunch of that stuff anyway, and that usually works just fine.

Can personal experience be wrong?

Seeing is believing? This classical optical illusion is a rabbit facing right or a bird facing left. There are hundreds of examples of optical illusions.

Some of our beliefs are deep-and they define us.

For as he thinks **in his heart**, so is he...(Proverbs 27:3)

Most of what we believe is fine, even without absolute proof. After all, it has kept us alive all this time. But how can we know what we hold as core beliefs? What we spend our thoughts, time and money on tells us what is most important to us.

Remember the Virtue Seesaw? So we can't prove our beliefs are all solid, still we find they are useful. Absolute certainty about things based on testimony and sense information is one extreme-just a bit of humility is called for there. At the other extreme is radical skepticism, refusing to believe anything until it is infallibly proven. A radical skeptic waking up:

How would you like to meet someone who could be your best friend? Or worst enemy? But it's up to you. Go to a mirror and say, "Hi. I choose from now on to have you be my best friend."

But isn't that selfish? Jesus said, "Love your neighbor as yourself." You have to love yourself, too.

Section 9

I Reap What I Sow

You've probably heard some expression that says you reap what you sow, Karma will catch up to you, or what goes around comes around. Most people get a little nervous about that, but it also works in the positive. Plant good seeds with random acts of kindness and you grow good plants for the future.

The eternal laws are not God trying to prevent you from having a good time. They are God trying to tell you how things work so you live a good life. Let's face it, he knows what you need to do to live a good life.

But it requires some effort on your part. Don't cuddle up with your baggage and false beliefs and waste your life. You may have kids or may have them someday, don't let the misery go on forever. Decide, "That's enough, it stops with me."

There is a story about about a Native American grandpa talking to his grandson:

We are all born with two dogs, a good dog and an evil dog. They are battling inside every man.
But grandpa, asked the boy, which dogs wins?
Grandpa answered: Whichever one you feed.

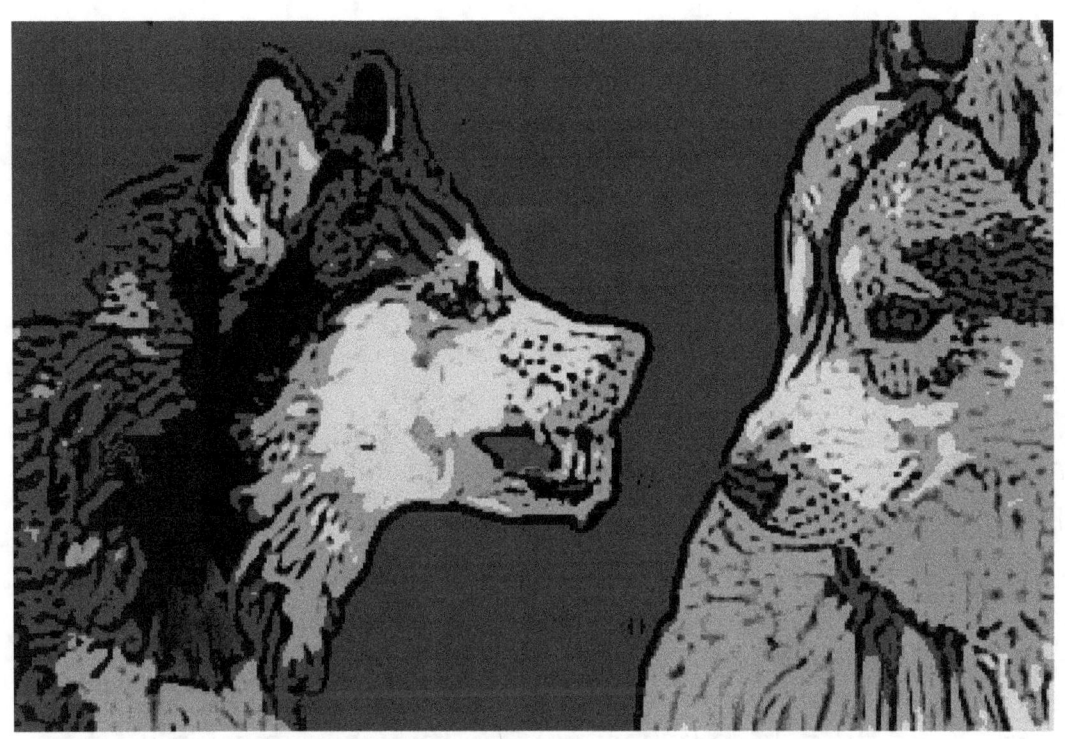

Trust is earned by trustworthy behavior over time.

"By their fruit you shall know them."-Jesus
Who was he talking about?

"Beware of false prophets. They come to you in sheep's clothing, but inwardly they are ravenous wolves. By their fruit you will know them."

Not by their clothes, or car, or looks? How about their smile or their handshake or smooth talk? Nope, you will know them by their actions over time, because one thing about fruit is that it takes time to grow. It is not a one time event, it is a process, and you, too, are producing fruit.

Trauma

If you were once bitten by a large dog or saw your mom stab your dad when they were arguing, you may feel very nervous when you see a dog or hear people arguing. You may not even remember the incident, but the panicky emotions will all rush back. You might refuse to get out of the car if there is a dog outside, even if he is friendly and wagging his tail. You may do anything to avoid an argument, either giving in or running away. The good news is, traumas can be healed, with the right help.

True story: A young woman, whose fiance had shot himself in the head in front of her, was enjoying a church picnic. A child popped a balloon and she fell to pieces, because the sound reminded her of the shot. Can you understand why that would happen? Could the other people understand, or would they think she was crazy?

Her friends understood and took her to a quiet place to talk. She desperately wanted to get rid of this uncontrollable reaction. Her friend offered to drive her by the house where the suicide happened. She could not do that. Her friend offered to drive her through the **town** where the suicide happened. She thought she could do that. One step at a time.

We all need help sometimes.

Chapter 10

We Forgive to Set Ourselves Free

After meeting many people whose lives are not working well, I noticed that each one had someone they needed to forgive. I also noticed this was the hardest work they undertook, and the most freeing.

Love and hate have this in common: They both bind you to a person.

If we are mugged by a stranger, we are naturally upset. But if we are harmed by someone we knew and loved, we are devastated. The biggest forgiveness task may be forgiving a parent, a person we had every expectation of protecting us. It happens. Fathers rape their daughters, mothers hatefully humiliate their sons. I will skip the true stories on this one, because they depressed even me.

A misunderstanding about forgiveness is that if we forgive them, they will never pay for their evil. But they will, and it may take a long time, but they will. I remember a particularly damaged victim helped by the metaphor of the Jesus jail.

Someone has done evil to you. First admit that it was evil, don't make excuses for the offender. You find that it preys on your mind, that hatred is eating away at you. So the damage continues. We forgive to set ourselves free from this hatred gnawing at our bones.

(Mentally)Take the offender, whom you have been guarding, and transfer them to the Jesus jail. In handcuffs. Turn them over to him. He can watch them from now on. He will do whatever is best. Then skip away free. Remind yourself when you think of the offense that the perpetrator is in custody in the Jesus jail. They are no longer your problem. You may have to remind yourself many times. But one day you will realize that you are free.

Another technique is to write to the offender. Tell them exactly what they did and how it has hurt you. Do not mail it. If they are dead, you can take it to the grave and bury it. Alternatively you can hold it up and declare, "You owe me nothing. I cancel the debt." Then burn the letter. Here is a form you might follow:

Dear ____,

You really hurt me when you _____. I hated it when _____. I wish that_____. This has caused me the following problems_____. However, I am stronger than before because_____.

Now, to yourself, say "Goodbye" to all that.

Yes, they owe you. They will not or cannot pay what they owe you. You choose to cancel the debt. You had no control when the offense happened, but you have control now. Use it to set yourself free.

Shelly had been grievously harmed by her husband. She cried. "I can't do it," she said. "I know it's right, but I can't do it." She also had a disease for which there was no cure. She made little cards and wrote the steps to forgiveness on them and read them at work and finally managed to get free. It took six months! By the way, her "incurable" disease disappeared, too.

We all have things to forgive, but some offenses go way beyond somebody leaving an empty milk carton in the fridge when you had just poured a bowl of cereal.

These are the notes Shelley took to work with her:

1. <u>Name the offense without making excuses for the offender.</u> They knew what they doing could hurt you deeply. If you don't honestly name the offense, what are you forgiving?
2. <u>Say it out loud: Lord, I choose to forgive _____ for _____.</u>
3. <u>Pray for the offender.</u> (When it comes back, pray again. And again. It will eventually stop coming back.
4. <u>Remember holding the grudge won't hurt them, but it could</u>

destroy you.
Unforgiveness is like drinking poison and waiting for the other person to die.

5. Remember it is a choice, not a feeling.
6. God said venegance is his, he will repay. He will do it better than you.
7. The best revenge is to choose to live a good life.

Forgiveness is not forgetting. You may never forget these big ones, but they will lose their sting.

Forgiveness does not require reconciliation. That is a case-by-case question.

Be patient with yourself. Love yourself. Keep working on it until you get free.

A good book by a secular psychologist is *Forgiving the Unforgivable* by Beverly Flanigan.

Section 11

I Have Done Some Rotten Things

The last chapter was about the difficult task of forgiving those who have harmed you. This one is about being forgiven for the rotten things we have done.

Dwayne and Rhonda were driving to granny's 90th birthday party, which was two states away and in a new house. Dwayne drove for several hours and turned off on exit 23. "Dwayne, I think you made a wrong turn back there," said Rhonda. She pulled out the map. "Yes, you made a wrong turn," she said. "I don't care what the map says. You don't have any sense of direction," Dwayne snapped. Rhonda was silent for half an hour then said, "Dwayne, can't we stop and ask directions?" "No, we can't. We'll lose too much time." Finally, it began to get dark and Dwayne pulled the car over and grabbed the map. "I've been going the wrong way. I'm sorry, Rhonda." They eventually got to the party, though they were four hours late.

People seldom do what they say they believe in. They do what is convenient and repent later. -Bob Dylan

What does it mean to repent? Like Dwayne, it means to 1. admit you've been going the wrong way, 2. turn around and 3. go the other way.

If you say you're sorry, but keep doing it, is that repentance? What if you feel really bad and say you're sorry with tears but keep doing it?

Most people have a pretty functional conscience, which nags them when they do something rotten. We understand that this is uncomfortable and say things like: "How does he even sleep at night?"

George Fox, an early Quaker from England, was visiting the governor of Virginia when a doctor said that Native Americans had no conscience.

46

Whereupon I called an Indian to us, and asked him whether when he lied, or did wrong to any one, there was not something in him that reproved him for it. He said there was such a thing in him, that did so reprove him; and he was ashamed when he had done wrong, or spoken wrong.

How do we get back on the right road, and sleep at night, and have peace? We might rationalize away what we have done and try to convince our self that it wasn't SO bad. Or that the bad feeling should be ignored or psycho-analyzed away. Or that these things should be graded on a curve. After all, we're not as bad as Stalin.

OR we admit it was wrong and turn around and go the other way. We admit it to God (who knew it anyway) apologize, and if we can, we undo any damage we may have caused. I find that what keep people away from God is that they are mad at God and need to forgive or they think he is mad at them and they need to be forgiven.

Does forgiving God sound absurd? Why might someone be mad at God?

Why is it so hard to admit we have done rotten things?

God forgives sins, not excuses.

Margaret was a caffeine addict. She actually got sick if she didn't have six cups a day. She gradually switched to decaf and he co-workers were encouraging. One afternoon, she got some decaf but put a shot of regular coffee in it, because she felt tired. A co-worker asked what she was drinking and she said, "It's decaf!" She started to feel bad about the lie. She accidentally knocked the coffee over on her keyboard. Then she went to her co-workers and told them it was regular coffee and she apologized for lying. "Why are you apologizing, it's no big deal," they all said.

When she spilled the coffee it was a mistake. When she lied, she sinned. When she admitted it, she repented. And she felt better.

The first two kings of Israel, Saul and David, sinned. Saul made excuses and David repented.

Saul said he brought the sheep from a raid, although he wasn't supposed to, "to sacrifice to the Lord."

When asked why he had not obeyed, he said, "I did! I did this and that and just brought the sheep back for ritual purposes."

Did he obey?

The prophet Samuel said obedience was better than sacrifice and turned to leave.

The Saul said, "O.K. I have sinned, but it was because I feared the people! So stay here and help me look good to them."

Does he still fear the people? Has he turned and gone the other way? He lost the kingdom, went crazy, consulted a witch and committed suicide.

David slept with the wife of one of his loyal soldiers. Then when she got pregnant, he arranged for the soldier to be killed in battle. When the prophet told him this, David said, "I have sinned." That's all. And David, it was said, was a man after God's own heart.

Did David offer any excuses?

Have you ever tried wrestling with your conscience? It says, "Don't do that. It's rotten."
You say, "Be quiet! Leave me alone." And the wrestling match begins.

You cannot ever win in a wrestling match with your conscience. If you "win" you reap the bad results later-and it if wins, it wins.

Section 12
The Big Questions

1. **Who am I?** A chip off the old block, a child of God, a pixel in the picture of the universe.
2. **Why am I here?** To grow your soul and flourish while you are at it.
3. **Where did I come from?** Ultimately, from the source of life.
4. **Where am I going?** Back to the source; if you so choose.

This book is for believers, which I assume you are. But maybe I'm assuming facts not in evidence. You become a believer when you connect with God. You grow as you stay connected to God. But how do you connect with God?

Many different ways. Try leaving your cell phone home, going for a walk and tell God, "God, if you are real, please show me." Be patient; his time is not the same as our time.

How I connected: I read a little booklet that said a few simple things. It said:

You sin. (I knew that.)
The wages of sin is death. (That's a bummer.**)**
You can't stop sinning by yourself (Not even with a New year's
                                      resolution?)
But the gift of God is eternal life. Gift?
If you could do right without God you'd just brag. (Would I? Yes.)

So do you want the free gift? I did, so I said this little prayer:

"Lord, I admit I have sinned and been apart from you. I accept your free gift of eternal life and I give you my myself. Help me stay connected to you."

Then I went out in the kitchen and asked, "So am I different now?" That's when the room lit up and I knew. I knew. That was over thirty years ago and I still know: God is good and I belong to him. Everybody's story is a bit different, though.

I did grow and I keep growing. I am flourishing on the road that winds upward.

I know.

You can know, too.

Je' Czaja

Je' Czaja founded and directed several non-profits serving disadvantaged children and their families, as well as winning several awards for art. She is retired and the mother of four wonderful kids. The Road Upward has been used successfully with groups of abused women, at risk youth, and prison inmates.

Other books by the author include:

The Magic Barn, volume 1 and 2
The Lord of the Beasts
As Sparks Fly Upward
Little Smarties Comics, Volume 1 and 2
https://www.amazon.com/Je-Czaja/e/B00IU4RWKE

And others.

www.ingramcontent.com/pod-product-compliance
Lightning Source LLC
Chambersburg PA
CBHW051943280526
45789CB00012B/2854